Printed in the USA

BPD In Their Own Words:
A Non's Guide

By Felicity Lard

Contents

V. Defying Reason

Borderline Personality Disorder or BPD has the astonishing ability to disrupt the lives of the people who suffer from the mental illness, as well as all the people around them. And the individuals who take the brunt of the personality hurricane are the BPs' significant others. An overwhelming majority of BPs are women, which means that the correlating majority of exes — or current partners trying to make it work — are men. That is why this book is devoted to helping current significant others and exes alike to understand what BPD is and why BPD women say the things you hear *ad nauseum.*

Being in a relationship with a BP is a harrowing experience, and most men have no idea what is going on during or what the heck happened to them after. All they know is that they fell in love with a fiery, passionate woman whose initial adoration quickly turned to disdain, and they found themselves doing everything in their power to get back the exciting, playful and intoxicating woman from the early days.

It is so important, moving forward in your understanding of BPD, that you realize the woman you were dating isn't a terrible person; rather, she did or does terrible things because BPD is a mental illness — a physiological imbalance in the brain — that disrupts her responses and makes her unable to regulate her emotions. She deserves compassion for what she is suffering, the same as anyone who is ailing from diseases both mental and physical.

But unless the BP is willing to seek mental healthcare, no matter what her significant other does or did, the outcome would be the same: she leaves a trail of destruction — emotional, physical, financial, etc. — in her wake, then seemingly moves on to the next guy without a glitch. That can be a devastating turn of events, but there are ways to mitigate the damage to your life (even after the fact).

This book aims to break the unhealthy cycles that occur when BPs twist and turn the conversations to their own benefit. If it is too late for you and your BP ex to remedy your relationship, at least let this book enlighten you to the true intentions behind the sayings she repeated over and over as you went through the same arguments again and again. She made you think you were going crazy — you were not. She made you think you were the bad guy — you were not. She seemed like the bad guy, and she was not. Though it was her mouth that was moving, it was BPD that was speaking.

I. The Victim

1. "You hate me!" or "Everyone hates me!"

The Reality: Whatever the truth of the matter, the BPD female is always keen to play the victim, and she will do it rather well with phrases like these. This serves an important purpose: she is attempting to live out a rescue fantasy, in which you rush to assure her that no one, especially you, hates her; in fact, it is just the opposite, and you probably poured on the flattery and words of adoration, just like she wants it. It feeds her narcissism and soothes her ego — at least for now.

The Root Cause: This part of her victim complex stems from events during her childhood, when she really might have been wrongfully accused of things she was too young to understand — like resentment from a parent. If the parent him or herself had BPD, a possibility because of the shared genetics, then it is entirely likely that the responsibility of having a child to care for was too great, and the parent's frustration and anger was taken out on the child. Thus, she grew up feeling marginalized, neglected, and resented — some BP women have *never* felt loved — and it internalized itself into her personality. No wonder she wants to be rescued with your soothing, sycophantic words — thanks to her childhood, she is paranoid that no one likes her, and her fear of abandonment as an adult runs high.

That childhood could very well have led to the BP's own feelings of self-hate, which she then projects upon you. It's easier to believe or throw accusations out, damning you for hating her, than to deal with her own conflicted inner turmoil.

Recommendation for Stayers: Instead of going over-the-top with your reassurances, answer her truthfully and matter-of-factly: "Of course I don't hate you. I love you." Repeat calmly and firmly. When it comes to everyone else's feelings, you can't know them, so instead, ask her if there is anyone in particular she wants to talk about — invite her to discuss it with you. Though you must stress boundaries — and perhaps her telling you how you feel is a no-no for you — you must be equally as understanding that it is her disease talking.

Recommendation for Leavers: Even though you didn't hate her and probably still don't despite everything you have gone through, her inability to move past her own self-hate and her constant need to be rescued could feel insurmountable. If she is consumed by both throughout your entire relationship — indeed, if it got worse as your relationship progressed, despite your best efforts — know that it isn't your fault. Learning to love herself is something that only she can accomplish when she is ready.

2. "You think I'm a terrible person."

The Reality: One of the most peculiar aspects of BPD is how the disease makes the BP woman swing upward from feelings of complete grandiosity down into a miserable depth where she is consumed with dislike for herself. When she is in these emotional pits, she tends to project these feelings onto her partner — *he* thinks she a terrible, worthless person. The end result is that her significant other falls all over himself to assure her that she is a wonderful, worthwhile person, the best person; but he usually ends up accused of patronizing or lying to her.

The Root Cause: BP women who grew up with BP parents (either mother or father) very likely were told — subtly or with jarring precision — that they were terrible, selfish people. Children are not supposed to be self-sufficient; they must, of a necessity, cling to their parents and look to their parents for all of their needs, including a home, food, clothing, and love. For a BP parent, that is a tall order, and resentful feelings (however much it is mingled with genuine love) reinforced throughout their childhood leaves now-grown BP women with more than a lingering view of themselves as terrible people.

Not all BP women grew up with BP parents, however; childhoods that were disruptive for other reasons, like a parent's alcoholism or drug abuse, parents who fought bitterly before, during and/or after a divorce, or a parent's own case of mental instability can all leave BP women feeling broken.

Recommendation for Stayers: Overacting either positively or negative when a BP tries to tell you how you feel about her is a no-no. Stay calm, and try something like, "I love you, and I do not think you are a terrible person. Can you tell me what makes you think that?" Get her to talk about it, so that she can learn how good it feels when her emotions are genuinely being addressed and her concerns validated.

Recommendation for Leavers: Always having to search for the right thing to say can feel like a losing battle, especially if you have never been with a BP woman before. It can seem like no amount of positive "propping up" has any effect on her. Sadly, that is the nature of BPD. If you find that you cannot convince her that you hold her high in your esteem, no matter how hard you try, it could be that this simply is not the relationship for you.

3. "Why does everyone always lie about me?"

The Reality: For BP women, life is viewed in black and white. She does not even realize it, but she is using words that express absolutes, like "everyone" and "always," in order to prove to her partner that she is 100 percent the victim of other people's opinions and gain both his sympathy and his unwavering support. This is also one of the ways BP women might justify vengeful behaviors — after all, she told her significant other about how people were always spreading lies about her, and so it is only fair, in her mind, that she strike back, usually in some impulsive and self-destructive way.

The Root Cause: BP women might suffer from intense anxiety issues, and as a result, can go through life quite paranoid, especially when it comes to what others think about her. She might think people are talking about her to begin with, but the BP penchant for projecting her own self-esteem issues onto others — in which she attributes her own thoughts and feelings about herself to the people around her — almost always takes a negative turn.

Recommendation for Stayers: It is important that you acknowledge her feelings; note that this isn't the same as validating them, which can only draw you into the warped BPD way of thinking, in which you almost always end up in an argument. Instead, try saying something like, "I'm sorry you feel that way. I know it can be difficult living in a small town like this, where everyone is in everyone else's business." Don't lie, but if you can, tell her or remind her of the nice things people have said about her. Do not get sucked into an argument with her about whether it's true or not; if she tries to argue with you, remind her of your boundaries and tell her you can talk more later when she is calm.

Recommendation for Leavers: The black-and-white way of looking at things (and people) can be one of the most difficult aspects of BP women, and it is one you will have to work at handling every day. On the plus side, you should get plenty of practice; but if you feel that you can't make headway and have a difficult time saying the things which prevent argument, then it might not be healthy for either of you to remain in a relationship.

4. "I cheated on you because of all the awful things I had to put up with while I was with you."

The Reality: Have you ever heard of rationalizing after the fact? It's when you give an answer, just off the top of your head or on impulse, but when pressed to come up with a reason, you simply make one up as you go along, whatever sounds best or most reasonable. For BP women, cheating is a very likely occurrence — the impulse-control part of their brains simply isn't as high-functioning as in non-BP people — and it is something they can get caught up in, with the rush of exciting emotions, for no other reason than it feels good and fun. Once their indiscretion has been exposed, however, saying something like this feels right to them, even if it isn't true. It certainly goes along with their tendency to devalue their partner after the initial idealization.

The Root Cause: As mentioned, BP women are wired to cheat. Well, they are wired to engage in any type of reckless, impulsive behavior, including sex, gambling, speeding, and other activities of that sort. But cheating especially is common, particularly in the 21st century, in which the Internet and cell phones have made meeting and setting up extracurricular rendezvous as easy as shaking hands with someone. Not only is the rush of doing something bad behind their partner's back a lot of fun — BP women who come from chaotic childhoods might have had parents who treated cheating in a nonchalant fashion.

Recommendation for Stayers: There is a saying: "Once a cheater, always a cheater." It's a bleak way of looking at someone, but it tends to ring true especially where BP women are concerned, simply because of the intense reward chemistry that courses through their brains when they do it (even more so than a non-BP person). That said, if you are open-minded and non-jealous, exploring different types of open relationship situations could provide a kind of solution. You both must agree on your own boundaries and rules, but it could eliminate the betrayal of cheating.

Recommendation for Leavers: If you find that an open relationship is not for you, no one could blame you — that is a situation fraught with all kinds of potential land mines, and it is not for everyone. If you have experienced her cheating before, you probably felt as though you weren't "enough" for her or you were doing something wrong, but you should rest assured that it was not the case; it was her BPD, and you shouldn't blame yourself, difficult as that might be.

5. "Nobody understands what I am going through."

The Reality: The BP woman certainly appreciates the advantages of casting herself as an isolated, tortured soul. Which isn't to say that she doesn't genuinely feel as though no one knows what she is experiencing — that is a very real possibility. But the disease creates in her a need to wallow, and more than that, to pull someone else down with her. This is a line that a BP woman might use in the beginning of the relationship, when she wants to hook herself a compassionate significant other who will take care of her (as she is desperately trying to assuage her fear of abandonment). Yet by not getting professional help, she is the drowning woman, and while she's not happy, her BPD urges are satisfied when sayings like this gain her attention.

The Root Cause: For a BP woman, it is easier to believe that no one "gets her," rather than deal with the fact that she pushes people away with her behavior. But inside, she is genuinely lonely, though lost, trapped even, inside her own head at the mercy of the unfolding of her emotions in whatever spectacular form it takes. Unfortunately, BPD isn't as nearly well known or as widely recognized as depression or bipolar disorder, and so she is actually telling the truth — few people understand BPD, how it works, or even what its symptoms are.

Recommendation for Stayers: Because it is true that you can never understand what exactly she is going through (unless you yourself have BPD), the very best thing you can do is get her to talk about her feelings and make her feel heard. The next best thing to do is try to get her mind off of the loneliness by engaging in bonding activities that bring you two together and allow her to create happy memories that she can think back on.

Recommendation for Leavers: You try and try to get her to talk about what she's thinking, but she shuts down or you end up in argument. Letting her just speak, no matter how irrational it sounds, might not come easily to you, and you find yourself interrupting her or pointing out how something she said doesn't make any sense. Unfortunately, this is not how you effectively communicate with someone who has BPD, and if you feel the frustration mounting because you cannot find any neutral ground, you might need to reassess the relationship.

6. "Why do you always get to be the nice guy?"

The Reality: Again, the BP woman is using black-and-white thinking to cast herself in the role of the victim, and her significant other in the role of the villain — a villain who is twisting her perceived truth and making her look bad by comparison. In her mind, no matter what she does, it never looks as good as what her partner does, and that's just unfair. However, the reality of the situation is that her BP is not under control and she is behaving the way she does almost against her own volition, which can be very frightening and cause her to seek out any number of excuses or justifications. Blaming her partner is an easy one.

The Root Cause: Growing up with BPD makes for one heck of a confusing and emotional adolescence, particularly if the BP woman grew up with parents who pushed blame onto her throughout the years. This in turn has made her feel as though she has always been persecuted for who she is while others get to bask in righteousness, and it's what she brings to her adult relationships, in which it seems like nothing has changed — she is always at fault, yet now it's always *his* fault for being "too good" or "the nice guy."

Recommendation for Stayers: There is no trying to use logic in this situation; you must simply rely on empathy and emotion to get you through. The fact is, this question is loaded, and it's designed to strike up an argument. Resist that temptation and keep the conversation even-keeled. Instead of telling her, "I do not always get to be the nice guy" — which will provoke an argument — try, "I'm sorry you feel that way. Would you like to talk about what has made you think this?" Get her talking, ask questions, and don't take the bait.

Recommendation for Leavers: It is terribly confusing when her BPD engages in splitting, and this is one of those sayings that probably left you feeling like you couldn't win. The truth is that you couldn't, not when it comes to BPD. If the necessary dialogue doesn't come to you over time, and the arguments keep getting worse, perhaps it is time to walk away before either of you gets more hurt.

7. "I don't know who I am."

The Reality: It is common for BP women to feel as though they are strangers to themselves, and after a particularly harsh rage episode, being caught cheating or perhaps ending up in prison — thanks to their inability to regulate their emotions — a BP woman might turn to this phrase in an attempt to try to divest herself of the responsibility of what has occurred.

The Root Cause: Sadly, there have probably been many instances in the BP woman's life in which she looks at herself and doesn't recognize herself or the things she has done. Some women very likely do realize that cheating or screaming at her significant other for no reason is not healthy behavior, but the impulsivity of BPD is so strong that she can't help herself in the moment.

There is also a very serious condition known as depersonalization, which BP women experience often, especially if they suffer from anxiety attacks. With depersonalization, the woman feels as though she exists outside of her body; for some women, it is as though they are watching themselves or living within a dream. While people who experience depersonalization often realize what is happening while they are in this state, feelings of helplessness, isolation, and confusion persist,

Recommendation for Stayers: Said when she is feeling very low, this could be an opportunity for someone who wishes to stay in a relationship. When a BP woman has reached the point at which she feels she doesn't know who she is, she could be open to having a discussion about taking steps that will make her feel better. But there are a few caveats: first, you must choose your timing well, because bringing up therapy at the wrong time could backfire spectacularly. Second, you should never try to tell her to do anything. Instead, say something like, "I have noticed you aren't feeling well lately. Do you think you might want to talk to someone about it?"

Recommendation for Leavers: Being with someone who seems lost or who cannot seem to take responsibility for her actions can be emotionally draining to the extreme. While she is not doing the things she does — the things that make her stop and say, "I don't know who I have become" — on purpose, without professional mental healthcare, the strain on both you and your relationship is very real. If you feel yourself startling to buckle under the pressure, perhaps you should consider going your separate ways. You can't take care of someone if you aren't taking care of yourself.

8. "I'm sorry, I don't know why I'm like this."

The Reality: You will probably hear her say "I'm sorry" many times over the course of your relationship with a BP woman, and the twist is that she is genuinely sorry, even though her BP gives her little control over the fact that much of the behavior she is apologizing for will occur again. Saying this phrase, though, makes her feel as though she is both atoning for what has happened and excusing it — hopefully with her significant other's full forgiveness and understanding. She hopes he will hold her, make her feel safe, and tell her, "I think you're a wonderful person."

The Root Cause: As we have discussed, there is a lot of truth in what she is saying when she tells you that she doesn't know why she does the thing she does; if her BPD is undiagnosed, then perhaps all throughout her life she has been considered a "wild child" or "the crazy one," and that was supposed to suffice as an explanation. Perhaps, as a kid growing up in a less-than-desirable environment, her own parents lashed out or raged at her, and then apologized afterward, crying while telling her they didn't know why they said/did the things they did. Ultimately, this could come to be a legitimate form of apology for her.

Recommendation for Stayers: This is another rare opportunity for those of you who want to make things work. If you feel that she is in an open and receptive mood, you can try to say something like, "I love you, and I want you to feel good about yourself. Have you ever considered talking to a professional therapist about your feelings?"

And then, instead of letting her wallow in sadness, why not suggest doing something to get her mind off of it? It could be as simple as taking a walk outside or running some errands.

Recommendation for Leavers: Perhaps her "I'm sorries" are genuine, and even though you recognize that she is afflicted with an inability to regulate her impulses and emotions, it could still be that you simply cannot bear another episode in which you find yourself abused by the things she says and does. It is well within your rights to decide if and when you walk away from the relationship.

9. "You never show me affection."

The Reality: This phrase is quite loaded and has a variety of purposes that makes sense in the BP woman's mind. First, it can be used as a way to justify actions like cheating or raging, an excuse after the fact, in which the BP woman is implying that because she is never held or hugged or kissed, her action — which is really the consequence of her BPD — is a valid one. It is also an indicator of her black-and-white thinking: you "never" touch her — never mind that you rubbed her back the other night until you thought your arms would fall off. Further, a phrase like this also stems from her fear of abandonment, which causes her to feel as though this is just the first step in you leaving her.

The Root Cause: Mental illnesses like BPD aren't necessary the sole result of "nurture" — or environment — but the environment in which people grow up can certainly exacerbate pre-existing mental illness, and the need for touch and affection from the time all of us are newborns is crucial. If BP women come from homes or childhoods in which they met with significant neglect, then chances are this is the type of thing they will say often as adults, because their whole lives they felt neglected, abandoned, disregarded; when a significant other enters the picture, BP women might have the unrealistic expectation that their knight in shining armor has come along — her rescue fantasy — but then reality doesn't live up to her fantasy, because you cannot be holding her all day long.

Recommendation for Stayers: Ask her something like, "What can I do to show you more affection?" It might be that she just wants more hugs throughout the day or wants a nice good-bye kiss when you head off in your different directions before work. If it is a simple request like that one, there is no harm in honoring it and, in fact, it really could strengthen your bond.

Recommendation for Leavers: One of the more difficult paths to read with BP women is divining how much is too much attention or affection.

Perhaps you are actually a very affectionate person, one who loves to cuddle and just hold your significant other, but because she no longer viewed you through the lens of the BPD's idealization, she shoved you off and said you were "suffocating" her. It feels like you can't do anything right, so perhaps you stopped trying all together. If you cannot find a happy middle ground in which both of your needs for affection are being met, perhaps it is time to consider leaving.

10. "I'll never binge/drink/gamble/get arrested again!"

The Reality: Anyone who loves an addict, no matter what the addiction, wants so badly to believe these statements. And the BP woman knows it, but no matter how earnest her sincerity, the sad fact is that BPD cannot "cure" itself and it's likely your girlfriend or wife will slip back into her old behaviors. There are a few reasons you cannot trust a statement like this. For one, it is black-and-white thinking — "never" is a long time and against very great odds. Secondly, it is a marked attempt to get you to let your guard down and not be so vigilant; it could be that she is already planning how to return to the impulsive behaviors that BPD rewards so pleasantly in her brain.

The Root Cause: Believe it or not, BP women probably have heard this statement quite a bit throughout their lives from parents or other family members. And as much as you want to believe it now, she wanted to believe it then. It gave her hope. Perhaps saying it in the present gives her that same hope for herself. Even if the promise was broken, the cycle of addiction/repenting feels normal.

Recommendation for Stayers: You must tread cautiously and be aware of the omnipotent presence of BPD in her brain. Those impulses and reckless behaviors won't just go away because she promised they would — the reward center in her brain is far too pleasurable. However, ask her about her plan to stay "clean," and if she does indeed follow through with those actions, take that as a good sign. Encourage her, but don't become her crutch.

Recommendation for Leavers: This is one area that makes it so surprisingly difficult for people to leave. It might seem like one trip to jail or one terrible car crash or one incidence of losing over $10,000 playing online poker would be enough to make anyone walk away, but many people stay, and then stay again, if only because of what they have invested — both emotionally and financially — in her wellness. You must be the one who sets the limits of what you are willing to endure and who must be strong enough to walk away when your boundaries are crossed.

II. It's All About Me

11. "My attention belongs to me."

The Reality: While BPD and narcissism are two different things, BPD women can certainly have narcissistic traits (without having full-blown narcissistic personality disorder or NPD). This saying often comes at a time when the BP woman is devaluing her partner; she has "split," and can only view her significant other in a damning light. This will throw him way off because previously she has been slavish in her devotion to him, and they have been spending all of their time together. Sadly, it is part of the BP woman's cycle of clinginess followed by pushing away (as a means for breaking down her partner).

The Root Cause: Often, parents and the home environment set the stage for behaviors that begin to appear in childhood and then blossom into full-blown disorders as adults. Perhaps the BP woman's own parents set an example by pushing her away as a child and declaring they didn't have time to give her attention. While it hurt then, as her brain developed with the BPD, it became an acceptable behavior for her now, particularly because of her abandonment issues — if she pushes you away now, you can't leave her later.

Recommendation for Stayers: React calmly and neutrally when your BP significant other says something to this effect; her BPD thrives on creating drama and chaos, and it wants you to either freak out and beg for her attention or leave her alone completely, so she can accuse you of abandoning her. Tell her you respect her right to self-reflection, but are there for her when she needs you. Repeat this often and actually be there when she reaches out to you.

Recommendation for Leavers: If you feel as though you are being pushed away and marginalized again and again, with no hope of getting out of the hater phase in any meaningful way, you should reassess your needs. Yes, your needs are valid and they should be met in a relationship that is mutual and loving. If that is not the case and there is no progress being made, you might have to make tough decisions concerning your future.

12. "People see me as bubbly and friendly, but I'm dark.

The Reality: A BP woman will say this during the hooking/bonding phase to give the impression that she is letting her new partner "see into her soul." BP women can make excellent use of this line to attract the compassionate rescuer because not only is he drawn into the mysteriousness of her hidden depths, he also wants to be the balm to her wounds. In fact, it strokes his ego a bit to think that he can succeed where others clearly have not.

The Root Cause: She is dark, actually, but not in the way she is thinking (which is in a romantic, exaggeratedly tragic fashion, like you might see in a movie). Undiagnosed BPD is not just alarming for the people around those who have it; it can be terrifying for the sufferer as well. Through depersonalization, BP women can feel like Dr. Jekyll and Mr. Hyde, and feel real terror as they realize they have no control over their impulsive behavior. This in turn causes them to strike out in panic, often at the people who care about them the most.

Recommendation for Stayers: Acknowledge what she says without judgment, because she really is reaching out to you for help. The main thing to keep in mind, however, is that you can give her real, constructive help, instead of the superficial kind that gets you stuck in the BPD relationship cycles.

Recommendation for Leavers: As much as you might want to, you cannot get angry at her for presenting herself one way and then taking off the mask; that is the nature of BPD. You can help her by being a constructive, proactive partner. But sometimes the task can be overwhelming, especially if you aren't completely healthy yourself. If you are striving to see the bright side, but find yourself being swept up in her darkness, you should consider taking a break and getting yourself well.

13. "I'm incapable of loving another human being."

The Reality: This is another saying that reaches out to the compassionate rescuer, whom she hopes will sweep her up into his arms and hold her there for as long as she desires it. A BP woman will use a phrase like this to hook herself a valiant knight who finds "fixing" an irresistible challenge. What makes this situation so twisted is that his heroic rescue does work — but only while the BP woman is in the lovey, "clinger phase." After that, all bets are off because BPD quickly unravels the happiness into pandemonium.

To that end, this phrase might be used when the BP woman is well into her devaluing phase and is pushing her significant other away (perhaps after she has cheated); it is said to manipulate the guy into doing whatever it takes to prove her wrong ("She really does love me, I know it!").

The Root Cause: Many BP women grow up feeling unloved, a climate that really has stunted her emotionally. It could begin as young as when she was a baby; if she lacked physical touch and bonding with her mother, her brain can be wired for difficulty later. Still, chances are good that she can feel and experience love, but the prospect is terrifying, and because of her BPD asserting itself as she navigates the waters of adolescence (when we learn through trial-and-error how to be with someone else) she ultimately doesn't know how to have a healthy relationship.

Recommendation For Stayers: It can be so scary for a significant other to hear a loved one say this, especially because they know the love between them is authentic. Believe it or not, she is not saying this to hurt you or because she truly means it — she is saying it because she is frightened. Talk her away from that ledge and ask plenty of questions, because she is reaching out to you. "What do you think causes you to feel this way?" See if you can ask leading questions that get her thinking about how to solve her emotional distress rather than wallow in it.

Recommendation For Leavers: This is a red flag, especially if you are the type of person who does not feel that he has lots of time, attention, and patience to put into a relationship. You have to understand that when someone says something like this, the relationship can be skewed — toward her — and you have to work very hard to achieve some kind of balance. If this is not something that you desire, perhaps you will have to look elsewhere.

14. "It's not me, it's you." or "It's not you, it's me."

The Reality: A statement like this is black-and-white thinking at its finest, designed to squarely lay the blame on one of the two of you. It's easier for a BP woman to just point fingers, regardless of where the blame lands (or what the truth is) because for her, any excuse is better than no excuse, particularly when it comes to excusing her impulsive, reckless behaviors. However, when the blame falls on herself, it is a manipulation to get her adoring boyfriend or husband to rush in with compliments and reassurances — "No, no, it's not you, you are perfection!" is what she hopes to hear.

The Root Cause: BP women who remain undiagnosed truly have no concept of what the real issue is, and you can see their panic in phrases like this, which seeks to assign all the blame for a huge amount of problems onto one person. This phrase usually comes as part of the hater phase, when the BPD compels her say distancing things in a manipulative move designed to keep him coming back. She pushes away, and he goes into a frenzy, wondering why the sudden shift of emotion, but willing to do/say anything to get his happy, idealistic relationship back.

Recommendation For Stayers: "It's not me, it's you" or its reverse is often preceded by an emotion — "I'm angry, and…" or "I'm sorry, but…" — so get her talking about what is really upsetting her. If she seems open and calm during the conversation, try steering her toward a discussion about how she — or both of you — might fix the issue.

Recommendation For Leavers: Being told that the problem is all your fault or all her fault can be dismaying, and if you cannot get her budge from that black-and-white thinking — which is very likely when BPD is left untreated — after a few failed attempts, you will have to consider if you are willing to keep trying to mend this rift in communication or move on.

15. "It's all about me."

The Reality: Narcissistic traits are apparent in statements like these, in which the BP woman is given to mistakenly believing that the world revolves around her. If not the world entirely, that is, at least her significant other should assume that his world now revolves around her, and she is essentially daring her partner to disagree with this new situation. If they have bonded well during the clinging phase, a boyfriend or husband who still has stars in his eyes over finding the love of his life will readily agree — at first.

The Root Cause: A BP woman might experience a lot of upheaval and chaos in her childhood and adolescence, including poor relationships with her parents, broken homes, and bearing witness to drug and/or alcohol abuse or other risky behaviors by her family members. To counter the experience of not having a lot of parental attention or affection, she will seek out relationships in which she can hook a rescuer and then let her BPD turn the tables. "It's all about me" is something she has rarely felt before and the experience is a heady one, especially if/when her partner really does make it all about her in an effort to return to the clinger phase. Gaining this kind of control over her significant other is both novel and addictive.

Recommendation For Stayers: Emphasize that her opinions and feelings do indeed matter, but make it clear that your opinions and feelings matter as well. Don't argue with her; just set your boundaries and be consistent. If you were giving and gracious at the beginning, when it came to meeting her terms, you can expect raging at this point when you put your foot down. But stay strong, stay calm, and show her that you are listening.

Recommendation For Leavers: Being unable to maintain healthy boundaries in terms of her narcissistic traits is not uncommon. What is going on in her brain is an alteration of the normal chemistry and behaviors of her different brain parts — that is no small thing.

Ultimately, struggling to keep your boundaries doesn't reflect badly on either of you, but you have to decide when enough is enough.

16. "I need to start being selfish and focus on me."

The Reality: While BP women don't mean to be selfish (it is often just a part of their illness), they do have a very limited POV — that is, limited to themselves and their needs/fears. The ironic implication here is that she is only JUST starting to exhibit those traits, but for her "own good." It is implicit that if her significant other objects, he is the "bad guy" and is holding her back, which is a symptom of her splitting that suddenly and abruptly renders him all bad.

The Root Cause: This phrase could be something that the BP woman heard growing up; now it is her turn, and she feels fully justified saying it because authority figures such as her parents used it. What it ignores is the fact that, while she does not mean to do or say selfish things, they are usually quite pervasive and obvious BPD symptoms, and they are something that her significant other will pick up on easily.

For Stayers: Let her know that you do support her when it comes to focusing on herself and bettering herself. BP women want to make their significant others into bad guys; resist the temptation to call her out on selfishness in the past. Instead, rephrase her words in a positive, constructive way: "I'm glad you are taking the time to focus on yourself! I'm here for you if you need support or someone to talk to."

For Leavers: Perhaps you begged her not to leave you out of her life; perhaps you said, "Fine," and left her alone; either way, you played right into the hands of what a borderline mind hopes to achieve. If you cannot find any other way to approach her when she is pushing you off, you might have to consider walking away for a time. Breaks can do the opposite of breaking you up — sometimes, they can be just what your relationship needs, and you can come back to her with a clear head.

17. "I don't need your money, help, or anything else."

The Reality: This type of phrase will come during the splitting phase of the relationship, when the BP woman is using the manipulation technique of creating distance to bring him closer. It seems paradoxical, but it works; by giving into her own fears of abandonment and pushing her significant other away, the BP woman takes the gamble that her partner will come on even stronger in an attempt to make amends and keep her. The deck is stacked in her favor. She is also emphasizing her own superiority, but at the same time might add, "…but I will take it because I deserve to be spoiled."

When a BP woman picks her mate, she chooses with an unerring sixth sense. She doesn't purposely go after certain men, the way a psychopath might, but rather gravitates toward "white knight" personalities, which she discerns by gauging his response to BPD words and actions. In the intense clinger phase, if she puts "I love you" out there after a few days and gets an "I love you, too!" back, she knows, subconsciously, she has found her guy.

And this is the type of guy who responds to "I don't need ANYTHING from you!" with "But I want to give you the world! A car, a new apartment, anything you want!"

The Root Cause: This phrase is certainly coming from a place of great insecurity; she is trying to sound strong, even though deep down she has abandonment fears. Perhaps past experiences using this phrase has taught her that her white knight can be controlled in this way, and again the reward center in her brain lights up with pleasure in a way it does not for a non-BPD person.

Recommendation For Stayers: It's a safe bet that she is reaching out when she says something like this. Ask her, in a non-pressuring way, if there is anything she feels she needs to talk about that would make her say this. Don't make the mistake of offering her more money, gifts, etc.

Approach her and attempt to help her overcome her emotional insecurities.

Recommendation For Leavers: It can be frustrating to hear someone say this and then take the money, help, etc. anyway. You have to set limits on how much of each you are willing to part with, and she has to know what those limits are. Be firm and follow through; hollow threats to leave don't solve anything. If she cannot abide by your boundaries, you must try to consider your own health and safety (emotional, physical and financial) first. This is one of the hardest lessons for partners of BP women to learn.

III. Emotional Blackmail

18. "You'll leave me one day, I know it."

The Reality: If your BP significant other uses or used this, she was using black-and-white thinking and overly dramatic language in order to get from you the assurance that she wants — that you will never leave her. She can then use these assurances later — "But you promised me you'd never leave my side! You said we were forever!" In her mind, it is evidence that you're just as bad as she thought.

It is also evidence that she is always right and she was right to voice these fears. But what is so extraordinary is that BP women also might, in extreme cases, harry her significant other to the point where he breaks down and leaves. And while she is heartbroken, she is also vindicated and clings to that feeling.

The Root Cause: Clearly, BP women suffer from extreme fear of abandonment perhaps more than those with any other mental illness, and BP women who suffer from narcissistic traits also may have a double wallop of this fear. BP women often grow up abandoned — by deadbeat dads, by absent moms, or maybe they were raised by their grandparents instead of their parents and only saw their moms and dads on occasion — before being left behind yet again. The fear that causes BP women to say things like this is real and often rooted in experience, but it is enhanced further by their illness.

Recommendation For Stayers: Instead of arguing with her about what could happen in the future (which no one knows or can know), ask her why she feels this way. Don't be baited into making promises you can't keep, but let her know you are here for her in the here and now.

Recommendation For Leavers: Don't give in to the temptation to lose your calm when she says something like this, even if you have thought about it. Assess each day as it comes and goes. Does she respect your boundaries? Is she actively trying to make positive changes? If you find that you can objectively look at her behavior and not see any improvement, despite the fact that you have made your boundaries clear, perhaps you need to separate.

19. "You'd better leave me for your own sake."

The Reality: This is a different approach on a similar theme. The BP woman is speaking from a place of fear and hurt; she is so afraid of abandonment that she would rather be the one who pushes her partner away than be left behind by him. This is her way of trying to be in control in a situation in which her BPD really has the control, but she doesn't know any other way to react.

A statement like this is also designed to *appeal* to the knight in shining armor, because what hero hears something like "You'd better not try that…it's impossible," and then doesn't make a glorious, heroic attempt to prove the naysayers wrong? BPD finds a way to manipulate with frighteningly penetrating insightfulness.

The Root Cause: A saying like this is caused by years of others abandoning her, starting from childhood. Perhaps her mother or father walked out. Perhaps they didn't physically leave, but emotionally withdrew their love and support; for a child, that is just as damaging. Even as the BP woman matures into adulthood, her past relationships were likely chaotic because of her illness and resulted in the significant other getting fed up and leaving. "This time", she decides, "I'm in control and I'm telling him go, before he can do it on his own."

Recommendation for Stayers: Ask her why she feels that you should leave. Speak from a place of honesty. "I have no intention of leaving you right now. I want to be here for you because I care about you and I want this relationship to work." However, this is one of those red-flag statements. If she has the clarity to say something like this, you should truly examine your health and emotional strength, because you are in for an unsettled ride should you choose to stay.

Recommendation For Leavers: Look at your own life first. Are you happy? Do you feel healthy? Only if you are truly happy and healthy (both mentally and physically) can you successfully be in a relationship with a BP woman. You might need to take a break and care for yourself before you can be with her. Or, you might realize that you are not equipped to deal with a mental illness as all-consuming as this — and that is nothing to be ashamed of.

20. "Why don't you get as upset about all this stuff like I do?"

The Reality: The BP woman, when she makes a complaint like this, is trying to get her partner to walk on eggshells for her. Her illness thrives on control, and getting her significant other to walk a tightrope — at her say-so — satisfies her fear of abandonment, at least for the moment (and it might last only a moment). Not only is she trying to control what you do and say, she is actually trying to control how you feel and what you think. It's a way of making herself feel safe.

The Root Cause: Again, this root cause of a question like this goes back to her abandonment issues. If she can subtly control or manipulate how you think and feel, she can feel safe in the fact that you will never leave her — or she can jerk you around however the impulses of her BPD stipulate, whether that's keeping you in the palm of her hand or pushing you off. Not having people strongly invested in her emotional well-being as a child causes her to overcompensate as an adult in a relationship. While nature plays a large part in her development, as ever, environmental factors also have a strong influence.

Recommendation for Stayers: Obviously, you are a separate human being from her, and you are allowed to feel a certain way or think a certain thing. You must implement boundaries in which you are allowed to react how you react, but with the understanding that you will do so with as much consideration for her as possible.

Recommendation for Leavers: If she cannot seem to accept your feelings as valid, no matter how many times you reiterate your "deal-breakers," the situation might continue to escalate every time you have a disparity in reactions. If she continues to attempt to tell you how to feel or how you should feel — particularly if she gets more and more agitated when you don't respond to her liking — you must remind yourself that you do have emotional needs and it is reasonable to desire a place of compromise. Remember: you are not the one with issues regulating your emotions.

IV. Blame Twisting

21. "Oh there you go
with that martyr complex again."

The Reality: This saying comes as part of hater phase, with the BP woman implying that her significant other is trying to play the victim, except the truth of the situation is that it's the exact opposite! Yet the BP woman feels like she is being attacked and/or criticized, and her BPD only knows one way of reacting: by trying to make her significant other feel guilty and responsible for the conflict between them instead.

Root Cause: One of the hallmarks of BPD is that a BP woman is unable to regulate her emotions because of the disorder. Accusing her significant other of being a martyr is also a way of expressing her own feelings of worthlessness, which have persisted since childhood. She never felt like she was good enough then, and now she is projecting those feelings onto her partner — putting words into his mouth, essentially, and implying that *he* thinks she isn't a good person, that *he* has to be the one to make the sacrifices because she is unwilling.

BPD is a disorder that causes people to warp and twist reality to fit their feelings, and when the BP woman believes her significant other is acting out with excessive emotion ("that martyr complex") — and she truly believes it — it allows her to feel both superior and in control.

Recommendation for Stayers: At this point in a conversation, very little will allow for a peaceable resolution. It is probably a good idea to just say, "I think we both need to calm down. Let's talk later when we have both had time to think." Arguing won't solve anything — it can make the situation far worse. Resolve to return to this discussion later if there are issues that still require working out.

Recommendation for Leavers: If her penchant for twisting and warping the situation truly gives you cause to believe that you are losing your own grip on reality, you might consider two things: seeing a therapist for your own inner turmoil, and taking a step back from the relationship to get your head on straight.

22. "Can't you just accept that some people are different? Can't I just be myself?"

The Reality: The BP woman makes a habit out of implying that the problem is that perennial bad guy, the partner, and not herself. She is devaluing him because he reacts negatively when she treats him in hurtful ways. Behaviors can include belittling him, criticizing him and everything he does, cheating on him, using his money in frivolous, impulsive ways, lying to him, or saying disturbing, overly dramatic things, like, "I wish I were dead. You'd be happy if I were dead." If he protests, he is trying to put a cramp in her style and keep her from finding her bliss or from being who she truly is.

The Root Cause: A saying like this is the BP woman's disorder trying to get her partner to accept the BP-fueled abuse. She wants control over him — control to make him stay right where he is, willing to do anything and everything for her sake. BP women often had to accept lines like this from a parent or family member, so it seems okay, even normal, to use it on someone else. She put up with it, she survived — no, she turned out *great* — so what's the big deal?

Recommendation for Stayers: You absolutely must make her understand that you love her, but not the way she treats you sometimes. So when you react to something she says or does in a negative manner, you are not criticizing her or saying she is a bad person, you are exercising your human right to have hurt feelings but still care about someone immensely.

Leavers: If you have set clear boundaries, where she must practice experiencing your hurt and pain without flying off the handle or trying to manipulate you into accepting her behavior, then you have a very real expectation that she will try to change and get better. It is up to you to gauge whether she is making progress with a sincere heart or if you are, sadly, wasting your time.

23. "Why can't you just be simple?" or "Why can't things be more simple?"

The Reality: The irony is that it is she — or, more precisely, her BPD — that is making things complicated. In her mind, it really is simple — YOU just don't get it. She needs you to give her space, so you do. But then you are abandoning her. So you come running back, arms open — and she rejects you, for being too "suffocating." You try again; you want to marry her. "But I'm already married," she cries. "How can you ask me to put all those years of hard work and love behind me? Why did you have to mess up everything with your love for me?" When in reality, she is the one who came on to you and made the first move. That is actually what made things complicated!

The Root Cause: BP women in the devaluing phase can be set off by anything. Their disorder is set to go off in rages at the slightest provocation. It makes no sense in reality, but the way their brains are wired, your desired behavior is straightforward to them. Essentially, every fiber of your being should be focused on them and their needs; they shouldn't have to actually ask for anything, because you should be so in-tune with their thoughts and desires.

Recommendation for Stayers: Ask questions that will turn this inquisition into a discussion that moves forward. For example: "How can I make things more simple? What do you need in order to feel as though the situation is straightforward?" Express willingness to talk it out, and try not to shut down just because things don't make sense or you seem to be going in circles.

Recommendation for Leavers: Everyone expresses at one point or another their wish for situations to be simpler, but BP women can take it to an unrecognizable, disjointed extreme. Be aware of the fact that her accusations could become more and more detached from reality, to the point at which you cannot do anything right; that is a sign that things could be taking a turn for the worse.

24. "By now you should know me well enough to know that I …"

The Reality: As mentioned, the BP woman is in such turmoil in her head that she can end up at a place of self-righteous indignation if her every whim is not anticipated and/or catered to. When she says something like this, she is expressing her belief that "You should have thought of that for me." But her mind changes so often, is so slippery and fickle, that her significant other is lucky if he can keep up. A true white knight, though, will hear this saying a few times and begin to believe that she's right — if he were a truly loving boyfriend or husband, he would be able to divine her dearest wish, her obvious intent, and act accordingly. She ends up manipulating him into beating himself down when he fails to.

The Root Cause: BP and narcissistic traits tend to prop up the BP woman's own sense of importance; she is programmed to believe that her needs should be the most important thing in her significant other's life. And she picks men with that feral sixth sense, hooking the ones who are most open — though they don't realize it and it is through no fault of their own — to being manipulated by a woman whose disorder attempts to control them.

Recommendation for Stayers: There is no arguing with a statement like this; instead, you have the change the tone and the direction. Try something like, "I feel like you want something from me that I'm not giving or doing — what is it?" Make the conversation about her expressing her needs in an honest, opaque way, rather than trying to manipulate you into doing something for her. Take things slow; let her practice simply saying what she wants and make sure you praise her accordingly for doing so.

Leavers: However, if she cannot pinpoint her needs, or if you feel that she is too changeable and not proactively trying to be frank (and if she starts "punishing" you for not reading her mind), you have the makings for a potentially toxic relationship. It is up to you how far it goes and for how long, but zero improvement in this area not a promising sign.

25. "You should have stopped me from..."

The Reality: The BP woman who uses statements like these before launching into a full-on attack for all the things you should have stopped her from doing is essentially telling you, "It's YOUR fault that I..." But you know that the truth is she cannot control her impulsiveness and penchant for reckless behavior. Even still, she legitimately believes the guilt should land on your shoulders. Blaming her significant other, after all, is easier than admitting responsibility or that she has a problem.

The Root Cause: This saying comes after the BP woman does something impulsive or reckless. It could be anything — driving drunk, stealing from a department store (and getting caught), blowing an entire paycheck on a new bag, or even sleeping with your best friend. Not only is she wired for instant gratification, her "rescue" fantasy has been shattered — you were supposed to rescue her from her vices, and you didn't.

Recommendation for Stayers: Having the weight of her actions on you is not how a mutual and healthy relationship functions (in case you needed reminding!). In order to create healthy space and a sense of personal responsibility, try saying, "It is not my job to keep you from doing certain things. You are an adult and have to make your own choices. Do you really want me bossing you around?" Accept that her blaming you will become a part of your relationship unless you put your foot down.

Recommendation for Leavers: As always, you have to make your limitations and your expectations clear if you want her to follow and respect them. If you feel you have done that, yet she continues to use you as a scapegoat and never takes any steps toward owning her actions, your relationship is veering steadily into unhealthy territory.

26. "I don't know where this is coming from. I'm not a nasty person. This is me attacking you, and I can see that. I do love you and sorry for being horrible to you. On reflection, I can see that you are creating a monster in me, and I'm sorry."

The Reality: What a twist! This meandering bit of conversation sounds like an apology…and then BAM! During hater phase, which is when a saying like this would pop up, she genuinely believes that *the things you do* to set her off are the problem, not her own incapability to regulate or control her emotions.

The Root Cause: Abusive people of all types use lines like this. The husband who hits his wife or the mom who screams at her child uncontrollably are both suffering from mental distress of some sort, and they both resort to statements that mirror this one: "*You* are the reason I hit/yell. Something *you* did caused me to react this way. If *you* hadn't done it, neither would I." So whether the BP woman grew up with an abusive father who hit his wife, or a mother who took her rage out on her children, the blame game is very familiar, and it feels valid, too.

Recommendation for Stayers: Don't take it personally, as tough as that is, when she says something like this. And try not to show your shock when she switches the whole game on you at the end. Take comfort in the fact that she is showing some empathy, particularly toward you. What can you do together to move forward? Make a plan and try to stick to it.

Recommendation for Leavers: Consider walking away if her accusations get worse; you know you aren't the cause of her behavior. If she persists in thinking so, it won't be healthy for a relationship. In healthy pairings, both sides are able to take responsibility for their actions to some extent (and they constantly strive to get better at it, instead of blaming each other).

27. "I should be able to express my feelings to you."

The Reality: Basically, the BP woman is suggesting that "I should be able to say whatever I want to you and you can't get mad because they are feelings (and I can't be wrong)." Bear in mind that she truly believes this. And while she is right to some extent — when she says what she's feeling, she isn't lying and she isn't wrong — that doesn't negate the hurt her significant other might feel when he hears that she "would rather walk on nails than have to sit through your family's Christmas dinner again this year."

The Root Cause: BPD and narcissistic traits share some important commonalities: they give the BP woman (if she has both) the illusion that her thoughts and feelings are better than everyone else's. It also makes her think that she is the center of the universe, and in particular, she is the center of her significant other's universe, bar none. This in turn leads her to truly believe that whatever she has to say should be allowed. And what's more, the combination of BPD and narcissistic traits can make a BP woman completely tone deaf to the possible fallout of her words. Far from worrying about whether or not she is hurting her significant other's feelings, she very likely assumes he will be gratified by her "honesty."

Recommendation for Stayers: She *should* be able to express her feelings, but with the caveat that she try to stay as calm as possible when doing so. You DO want to know her feelings, it just hurts you when she rages or blames things on you. And you should make sure that she agrees with the fact that you also have feelings, are allowed to be hurt, and should be able to express that pain before moving on.

Recommendation for Leavers: It is one thing when she has a few foot-in-mouth situations, but is working actively to correct it. It is quite another, however, if she is taking no steps toward censoring the more hurtful things that come out of her mouth. Use your best judgment if her "feelings" become overly abusive and out of control, to the point at which she might as well be physically hitting you.

28. "Why do you always argue with me?"

The Reality: A phrase like this is the BP woman's way of forcing the blame onto her significant other for the turmoil and arguments in their relationship. The ironic thing in this situation is that she's not entirely wrong; you do argue with her (you're hard-pressed not to try and stand up for yourself at first), but she is the one actually picking the fights, twisting words, and trying to circumnavigate logic and/or the truth.

The Root Cause: It is always easier and more desirable for BP women to accuse significant others of being difficult or picking fights than to acknowledge that they have a hard time using logic. Some BP women might very well be quite logical in other parts of their lives, like at work (where they cover their BPD well) or when putting together furniture at home, but they cannot overcome the wiring in their brains for strong, impulsive, and emotional outbursts that inevitably lead to conflict with their partners, and may well create rifts with the rest of their family, too.

Recommendation for Stayers: Protesting and trying to convince her of your "side" will create more of an argument. Acknowledge her feelings — she feels exacerbated and undermined. Let her know you're willing to hear her out, if she is willing to hear you out. There has to be some level of mutual understanding, and she must agree that in order to have a healthy relationship, you have to be able to agree to disagree sometimes.

Recommendation for Leavers: Try to compromise as often as you can (with both sides giving a little bit), but if the middle ground you seek never surfaces, it is time to take a step back and re-evaluate what makes you happy in a relationship. She has to be willing to make an effort — relationships can't exist one-way.

29. "Why do you always create chaos?"

The Reality: "Why do you always create chaos?" is likely a reaction the BP woman is having to her significant other getting upset about something she has done as a result of her BPD. She is attempting to sweep her behavior under the rug and instead focus on his reaction as the main event — how dare he have a negative reaction to something that she has done! This also serves to break down his self-confidence — the white-knight type of male gets sucked in, and then as she distorts his reality, he can really start to believe that he's a bad guy who goes around making trouble. But the truth? It is without a doubt the BP woman, since the chaos wouldn't exist without her disorder.

BP women with narcissistic traits will do anything to keep the blame from landing on their own shoulders, including distortion of the truth; this is the nature of gaslighting. It is important to note that the BP woman genuinely believes that her significant other is the source of the chaos, not herself; when she accuses her partner of making trouble, she is being sincere. What is also happening is that she is projecting her own behavior onto him, something BP woman do well and often. BPD thrives on chaos and disrupting others' emotions.

Additionally, this could also be something that a BP woman's parents did to her: projecting the blame onto an innocent child who cannot defend herself, which then added to the environment that nurtured the woman's BPD.

Recommendation for Stayers: Don't let yourself be drawn into an argument over who is at fault. If you need to just end the conversation because it is getting nowhere, do so. Try, "I would prefer to just end the chaos right here and now. Perhaps we can have a calm discussion about this later. I am going to head to the gym." Put some distance between the two of you if need be.

Recommendation for Leavers: How much is too much gaslighting? There will be a different threshold for each person, so only you can decide if you absolutely cannot get anywhere positive or find any happiness in the relationship.

30. "I've been going to counseling for years to get help, but you're the one who still won't change."

The Reality: Perhaps the BP woman is telling the truth (with little exaggeration); maybe she really is in therapy and is trying to work through her disorder. But using a statement like this is giving into the BPD, as she is attempting to simultaneously justify BPD actions and blame her significant other for continuance of them. Her way of thinking is that she's the one making the grand gesture of going to therapy; he's not even doing that, and since their problems are the same and the fights won't stop, he must be at fault.

The Root Cause: BPD treatment requires constant vigilance, and while people can have success, it is a difficult, slow journey — this is the chemistry of her brain she is trying to overcome! Slow progress can make the BP woman feel as though she needs to blame her significant other for "holding her back." Projection will likely always be an issue for a BP woman as well, because the tantalizing ease of placing the guilt on him, rather than owning up to how much work she still needs to do still sets off the "reward" button in her brain.

Recommendation for Stayers: Show appreciation for her willingness to get help for so long. That is a huge step for a BP woman to make, to the point where the vast majority of BPD sufferers will make it their life's work to avoid admitting they have a problem. The BP woman going to therapy or counseling is huge. Now, to meet her in the middle, you can to make a "change for the better" plan — she can do a/b/c/, you will do x/y/z. You unite and grow closer with the knowledge that you are both in it together and are both striving to be better.

Recommendation for Leavers: Monitor your BP significant other for sincerity and signs of improvement. Some people choose to keep a little journal in order to view the effects of the disorder from a factual, non-emotional place. If her distortion of reality — that you are the root of all her problems, not the hold on her brain that BPD has — is too severe and unchanging, and you can see it on the page right in front of you, perhaps you should consider other options moving forward.

31. "If I'm such a terrible person, then why do you want to be with me?"

The Reality: When your mouth starts moving with a critical tone, your BP partner is hearing that her significant other is upset, but instead of hearing your exact words, her brain is translating it into "I think you are a terrible person." This makes it easy for her to twist the situation so that she can accuse him of being the crazy one for thinking she's the bad guy (which he doesn't, and she is projecting her black-and-white thinking onto him) and yet still being with her.

The Root Cause: BPD is marked by mood swings, including shifting opinions of the self. BP women can have narcissistic traits (particularly when it comes to comparing herself to her significant other), and yet still swing down low and find little self-worth and much emptiness (caused by lack of positive encouragement as a child). Thus, she is projecting her own poor self-esteem, her long-held belief that she is a terrible person, onto him. It is certainly part of her fear of abandonment — an ever-present, yet generally incorrect view that everyone she loves will leave her.

Recommendation for Stayers: Separate the things she does from who she is. Try telling her, "You are not a terrible person, but sometimes the things you do hurt me. I'm allowed to feel hurt, yet still love you and want to be with you." You might have to repeat this dozens of times before she starts to believe you or understands what you are saying.

Recommendation for Leavers: There may come a point where she breaks off from reality so harshly that she actually begins to berate you or belittle you for staying with her. It's up to you how much of this you will take, and how firm you are in putting your foot down and declaring that you won't put up with this particular behavior. It is also entirely your call in deciding if/when you have had enough.

V. Defying Reason

32. "I hate you. I love you." On repeat.

The Reality: Idealization and devaluation are part of a cycle that wears down the BP woman's significant other, eating away at both his sense of self-worth and his sanity. The whiplash he gets from hearing "I hate you," followed by a brief pause (of minutes, of hours) and then "I love you!" serves to put him in a low, unhappy place, then build him up, and tear him down again. It makes him emotionally dependent upon the BP woman, so that his emotions — even his thoughts — are eventually dictated by her disorder.

The Root Cause: The "I love you, I hate you" cycle is something the BP woman might have heard a lot in her childhood; mentally ill parents (whatever their illness, be it depression, bipolar disorder, etc.) swing between moods of intense love and intense resentment, though none swing quite as severely, or in such short order, as those who have BPD. When a BP woman goes through this process, she is attempting to gain control of the situation because of her fear of abandonment. Instinctively, she feels that if she can do what it takes to keep her significant other totally devoted to her, she can find some measure of safety.

Recommendation for Stayers: You are allowed to feel hurt and to tell her so. Try: "It confuses me and hurts me when you say these things back and forth." Suggest this as a boundary: she is allowed to feel what she feels, but she doesn't always have to say it out loud. Perhaps she could try journaling? Lots of people with zero personality disorders sometimes feel that they could strangle their spouse, so it's not an uncommon phenomenon to go back and forth a bit. But in the case of a BP woman, she must learn not to let passing, momentary mood swings have such a marked effect on her relationship.

Recommendation for Leavers: If she can't seem to gain any control over the impulsiveness of her mouth, know that you don't have to put up with being verbally jerked around. If you have mutually agreed that she will try to stop saying negative things out loud (toward you) the second they pop into her head, yet she doesn't improve or seem to care, know where you draw the line and follow through.

33. "I never loved you."

The Reality: "I've never loved you" is designed to hurt your feelings, but not because she genuinely wants you to feel pain. BP women might be unreasonably unstable, but they rarely behave because of mean-spiritedness or maliciousness; instead, she might say this right after a breakup because she wants to feel like she had the upper hand in the relationship. This might also come out of her mouth during the recycling process, when she is trying to pull you down after building you up with affection.

The Root Cause: This saying really comes back to her fear of abandonment. As a child who was abandoned — perhaps over and over — she learned that putting up walls makes you feel safer. She can feel safer now because she obviously wasn't abandoned, even if she and her significant other did break up; that is to say, in her mind, she "abandoned" him emotionally first, so even if he broke it off with her, she had decided they were already finished — he just didn't know it.

Recommendation for Stayers: If you are thinking about getting back together, or if you have just gotten back together, stay calm and don't burst into tears or make a scene, which is the type of chaos that BPD thrives on. If you have just gotten back together and are having an argument, try saying, "That makes me sad to hear, because I did love you and still do. But if you are willing to work on us and let love grow now, so am I."

Recommendation for Leavers: If you are thinking about breaking up already, this can feel like the straw that breaks the camel's back. Don't fly off the handle, hurtful though it might be. Remind yourself that she is speaking from a place of *hurt and fear*, not maliciousness. Ask yourself whether you think she is sincere about this or not and proceed accordingly.

34. "Being right is more important to you than loving me."

The Reality: This is an attempt to avoid blame in the relationship by the BP woman. She is basically saying, "We argue all the time and have problems because *you* can't be wrong." Not only is this playing the blame game, she is seriously projecting; while remaining ignorant of her own inability to admit that she's wrong, she is pointing the finger at her partner for the exact same offense. She is also appealing to his inner white knight. What gallant wouldn't respond with, "No, no, you're wrong! Loving you is the most important thing to me!"?

The Root Cause: Pinning the blame on her significant other — when it is ironically the precise opposite of the truth — is easier than acknowledging her own role in the nature of the stormy, argumentative relationship. BP women truly cannot see their own behavior for what it is. Someone is to blame, but it surely can't be her, which goes back to any narcissistic traits she might have.

Recommendation for Stayers: No matter how difficult it is, don't let the argument drag on by attempting to use logic or reason with her. Instead, tell her as calmly as possible that because you care about her so much, you must insist on healthy boundaries so that you are the best possible version of yourself and you can be there for her in a constructive, proactive way. The sad fact is that no matter how hard you try, you can't rescue her. BPD's chaotic effects must be strategically minimized by a team of people, including the BP woman, any therapists or counselors she sees, and the people who love her.

Recommendation for Leavers: If your relationship begins to become a never-ending parade of these no-win sayings from her, her disorder clearly has too much of a stronghold on her and it can drain the life out of you if you let it. If she cannot stop twisting and turning the conversations so that the blame is all yours, decide whether an exit strategy is worth developing.

35. "I want you to marry me as soon as possible. But I'll stop with my new boyfriend when I am better."

The Reality: BP woman love to attempt to have their cake and eat it, too. This saying will commonly come out at the beginning of a new recycle, when she has picked up with an old boyfriend. She is saying that she needs all the love and support she can get, and is implying that if you deny her that, *you* are the one being selfish. She'll justify her continuing relationship with a different boyfriend by telling you, "YOU'RE the one I want to MARRY!" And if you can't see the difference, that's your problem, because it all makes sense in her mind.

The Root Cause: Narcissism and an overinflated ego can lead the BP woman to feel as though she deserves a special pass. A sense of entitlement is common with BP women, yet they rarely recognize it as a departure from the norm; you would never hear a BP woman say, "I know it's a bit excessive, but..." This is one aspect where they do little rationalization. BP women also suffer from a crippling fear of abandonment, and this could be a way of safeguarding themselves with multiple partners, so that if one relationship fails — and she just knows that it will — she has someone to fall back on.

Recommendation for Stayers: You have to decide what your deal-breaker might be. Are you comfortable with her having a relationship with someone else? Can you set boundaries in which they are permitted to be in contact, but only as platonic friends? Do you have a way of making sure they stay platonic? The chances that the relationship is sexual and will stay sexual are very high, so you must proceed with caution.

Recommendation for Leavers: Chances are also good, barring some catastrophic event, she will not stop seeing this other boyfriend, even if you marry her. However, you get to say how much is too much, and it will vary from man to man. If monogamy is important to you, clearly outline your needs and the consequences, and then follow through if she oversteps herself. If you have a more nontraditional outlook on relationships, perhaps she is allowed to have other sexual relationships, but there are rules — no lying, always use protection, etc. — and if she breaks any, you are within your rights to walk away.

36. "I never lied in my life."

The Reality: Incredibly, the BP woman might truly feel as though she has never told a lie. So while you might think (or know) it's a lie, she doesn't necessarily recognize that as such. This is a good example of the type of black-and-white thinking ("I'm the perfect good girl!") that is so prevalent with BP women, and there's a touch of gaslighting — she believes it so sincerely because of the BPD's distortion of her reality that you begin to wonder if maybe you're the one going crazy, and you end up second-guessing yourself. Such a bald and untrue statement as "I never lied in my life" is meant to throw her significant other's mind into total chaos.

The Root Cause: Narcissistic traits and BPD again work together to create an overinflated sense of self. But there's more to the story: the BP woman needs to feel like she is okay — in the face of myriad evidence otherwise. And if she can distort the reality that her significant other experiences, convincing him that everything she says is the truth, she can simultaneously control him and further convince herself — since he is convinced — that she is indeed the perfect good girl who is just fine.

Recommendation for Stayers: Instead of straight-up accusing her of lying, try more general statements like, "Everyone lies at one point or another." If she is saying this because she feels that someone is accusing her of something, ask her, "Do you feel you are being misunderstood or misrepresented somehow?"

Recommendation for Leavers: BPD is shockingly powerful, creating chaos and confusion wherever it goes in the person of a BP woman. Many men — strong, iron-willed men who were previously masters of their own universe — get swept up in it and carried away on the tide of their significant other's disorder. If you are seriously questioning your own sanity and grip on reality, or if you catch her in lies and yet she persists in insisting that she is honest to fault, you need to do whatever it might take to keep your own mental health up to par. Some men date BP women so frequently (or date one or two with such intensity) that they begin to exhibit BPD behaviors themselves.

37. "Stop psychoanalyzing me with your psychobabble."

The Reality: The BP woman is essentially saying, "I'm fine, and if I'm not fine, it's only because you are driving me crazy!" She is gaslighting, implying that her significant other is the one with the problem; he is the one trying to make a big deal out of nothing, trying to "read between the lines" when there is nothing to read, while she is the one who is even-keeled, perhaps even the victim of his vehement and misguided persistence in the belief that there is something that needs to be fixed with her.

The Root Cause: Most people with BPD will deny to their last breath that there is anything wrong with them, and this is one of the ways they push off concerned partners. Admitting they have a problem or an illness is almost scarier than how they feel when they can't control their emotions, as if admitting to a mental health issue makes their entire house of cards fall down with one swoop. They prefer to live in the illusion because it feels safer to them.

Recommendation for Stayers: Don't press the issue; that will only make things worse. Try something like, "I'm only concerned because you seem more stressed out than usual. Is something the matter?" Make it about the here and now, not the past or the future. And judge your timing wisely.

Recommendation for Leavers: Resisting psychotherapy is extremely common among BP women, but only you can judge if her illness has become so pervasive that it is affecting your life in markedly negative ways. If it gets to the point at which her behavior is hurting your relationships with your family members and friends because she is increasingly clingy, or threatening your job stability because she shows up and creates scenes, you have some difficult decisions to make.

38. "How much do you love me on a scale of 1 to 1.7?"

The Reality: The BP woman is "testing" her significant other's devotion, usually during the hater phase, when she has turned nasty and devaluing. Yet saying something like this, in one of those rare "sweet" moments when her significant other starts to think maybe the woman he fell in love with is back, is her way of appealing to his knight-in-shining-armor complex; she knows he will swoop in with an answer of, "A MILLION! A BILLION!" And so her need for security and safety is satisfied (but for how long?).

The Root Cause: And that's what it is. It's about constantly needing to remind herself that she is safe, while constantly reminding him that he is her number one fan (and he'd better not forget it). A child starved of love growing up is also going to yearn for it and need constant reiteration as an adult. Once a BP woman has discovered that certain men can be hooked and made to say or do whatever she wants (when she learns the potent effects of idealization/devaluation) she will perpetuate her behavior on impulse to feel as though she is control and secure.

Recommendation for Stayers: Instead of rising to this very obvious challenge, try something like, "There is no measurement for my love. I could never confine it with arbitrary numbers." You want to stop this line of questioning in its tracks because it is going to lead you into unhealthy territory (you as a white knight, her as a damsel in need of rescuing).

Recommendation for Leavers: Getting "tested" over and over can be frustrating, especially when you feel like there is nothing you can do to prove that yes, you truly love her. Consider walking away if she ignores your requests for an end to questions like these or it only makes her ask them more often (perhaps because she is involuntarily trying to see how far she can push you).

39. "I never stopped loving you;
I just stopped my relationship with you."

The Reality: The BP woman is trying to explain away the fact that you broke up before (perhaps many times). Her love was constant, she is saying, but outside circumstances made an official relationship impossible. She could be using this as an excuse for why she started seeing someone else or cheated (with the implication being that it's not as bad as YOU might be making it out to be, because she still loved you!). This is also her way of rewriting history after it has happened, something many BP women do. But they aren't just twisting the truth, while knowing deep down that they are being purposefully manipulative; once the BP woman is confronted with a new, contrary situation, she earnestly and sincerely believes in all the rewrites she must apply.

The Root Cause: A phrase like this is an attempt to cover up the real problems. "I just stopped my relationship with you" glosses over a whole trove of BPD-related issues, from lying, to cheating, to emotional outbursts, to verbal abuse, etc. "I never stopped loving you" is, in her mind, more important than all of those things, and she wants her significant other to believe it, too. If she can bring him around to this line of thinking, it will cover all manner of behaviors in the future as well. So if she cheats or gambles away large sums of his money, she has to do even less work in convincing him that it's not so bad — he is already telling himself, "But she loves me, and that's what really matters."

Recommendation for Stayers: Tell her your limits in terms of what behaviors you will tolerate and what you won't. Explain to her that just because she never stopped loving you, it doesn't change the fact that you feel hurt by what she has done.

Recommendation for Leavers: You can stop the cycle of recycling before you get pulled in again if you so choose. Does she sound sincere? Do you still love her? Does your love outweigh your fear of going through the drama that her BPD creates? Perhaps "yes" to all of these questions. But if "no," you have some thinking to do before you can let yourself get involved in this relationship again.

BPD In Their Own Words: A Non's Guide

40. "Just because I didn't tell the truth, doesn't mean I lied to you."

The Reality: "Selective truth-telling" can be a good thing when applied in general social situations in which one wants to avoid TMI, but when it comes to BP women, it's more likely that her practicing selective truth-telling is an attempt to cover up an all-out lie. Not only can she not truly see the lie for what it is, she is attempting to reason "minor" infraction away — maybe she'll go on to say, "I hinted strongly for you, you should have picked that up," or something similar. How could you fail to guess that "grabbing drinks at happy hour" meant "impulsively hooking up with her coworker in the bar restroom"?

The Root Cause: BP women are controlled by their impulses and their need for instant gratification, and in most cases that need is to deny that they are capable of doing anything truly bad or hurtful to someone (especially someone they love). This is part of their splitting tendencies, where they are all good (and their significant others are usually all bad). The reward center in their brain is simply wired differently. While most people get pleasure out of pacing themselves and earning a goal slowly, BP women experience an addictive rush of happy feelings when they want something and immediately get it. And selective truth-telling is an almost natural reaction after the fact.

Recommendation for Stayers: Even if you know she lied, remember that she did it because of a fear of something. Perhaps she's afraid you'll leave her if you find out. If you want her to be more honest with you, you will have to make sure she feels safe enough to confide in you. Only then can you begin the process of working through whatever she lied about.

Recommendation for Leavers: While your knee-jerk reaction might be to dump her for betraying you, you must also keep in mind that BPD — and the fear it causes — is what motivates her to not tell the truth. If your attempts at communication and creating an open, honest dialogue fail, then perhaps it is time to walk away.

81